The Last Thing Is Longing

The Last Thing Is Longing

Michelle Rebidoux

RESOURCE *Publications* • Eugene, Oregon

THE LAST THING IS LONGING

Resource Publications
An Imprint of Wipf and Stock Publishers
199 W. 8th Ave., Suite 3
Eugene, OR 97401

www.wipfandstock.com

PAPERBACK ISBN: 978-1-6667-3485-0
HARDCOVER ISBN: 978-1-6667-9121-1
EBOOK ISBN: 978-1-6667-9122-8

.   OCTOBER 29, 2021 1:37 PM

For Sri Chinmoy

Contents

WE TWO

We two fight over
who is to be lover
and who beloved.

BUBBLES

Once on the road
to the sea in the morning,
with the sun ablaze behind me,
laughing in its canopy,
I found suddenly that
misplaced part of my belly
where life brews up its potency
as living bubbles of joy.

At the top of the hill I found it
and was wild
with that bright first glance
upon the wide blue water.
I found it in the intimacy
of a moving depth
that promised as a mother
to keep secrets of a daughter.

And one bubble rose up, then,
so high within me
that quick as springtime
it spawned a song and a prayer—
a prayer for Your forgiveness
for the day of reckless play,
a song of heartful gratitude
for the same already given.

Or, in any case, a song
for that rare gift of the bubbles,
and forgiveness
for my exorbitant hunger for them.

THE GREAT ENVISIONING

Listen, my friends,
it is not a small thing,
no heart's lyricism,
no enchantment of songing.

When once the decision
is definitively made,
there is no going back upon it
without ruin—body, mind, and soul.

There is no possibility
of dragging a few oddments along.
They are incompatible with the road,
yea! with every cell of being

there in that beckoning place
towards which one leaps now
with bounds of verve and elegance,
like a deer given (almost) wings.

For so has your life at last
been marked indelibly,
and all your members set
on the path of their translation,

when once you make that choice,
and it is confirmed by those
whose business is to fashion you
according to the great envisioning.

THE DECISION

The time for whispering ends—
the decision approaches.
Where will you go, my desire, where?
With what hope
might you in trembling venture forth,
a refugee in exile
from out of this heart when I have
sent you away, saying:
Did you forget that you would be
wrested from me in time?

What was intimacy sweet
has soured from this summons.
No longer have you any home here,
nor elsewhere in sight,
yet pray you may be ever welcomed
there where you land!
I shall soon enough hear some news
of your arrival and
that unknown place's appointment of you,
your new berth,
and then must I decide.

Shall I without sleep launch forth,
without retirement, or shall
my solitude utterly destroy
all that I had hoped beyond hope
for you as sacrifice?
Where, my child, where shall you go?
—if not ... *à-dieu* ...

THE TEACHER

As though in a wind-swept, vasty field
he looked ahead and saw a road for me,
pointed with eyes silent, then turned back;
he left me to follow it on my own.

Now I, in the quickening of his investment,
must walk surely in that direction alone.
Would it not trouble his heart if I did not?
Would I not have betrayed his promise?

But, too, would it not trouble my own if,
when I am gone, he did not e'en once turn
to look after me from afar and smile?
There let his silence compel a vigil of the wind
carrying to me the hopes of untold futures
his because they are mine—*him because me!*

OLD PINE

And so grows
the precipitate vine.

All this time,
given longsome time
that you've forgotten
you've called—
promised my heart,
yet now sleep,
left hunger of heights here!

Even Justice finds you
nowhere near
that it might gather you back,
decree
to unhide from me
whom you've borne,
make you recognize
this life you've torn!

O! old pine! Old pine!

Enough!
Now you must remember.
I've given you
countless days' tears;
I've given you
all but this of my fears:
I'm still too young
to leave home.

LITTLE HEART

Little heart,
you are young—
your tearful pangs
know nothing
of all songs sung.

Do you not
want something
more than this
in your hands,
great gifts
of unknown lands?

Little heart,
learn patience!

MOTHER'S SANCTUARY

There in some sweet, gentlest intimacy
behind the veil did I behold your handmaids
tenderly smiling, unmurmuring, patient
with timelessness, knowing no expectancy,
no frontier. —How I entered, mother,
into your compassion's chamber I know not,
but there, all suffering left me—
some ancient memory unrecollectable called me home.
And as love does not allow a past so distantly past
to be grasped as past presence,
this body of your earth's longings yielded up
its heart's hands and breathed release.
Mother, there, in your compassion's chamber
in your handmaids' care, it knew peace.
Whatever hope was in my soul before this time
became yours, and it endures in you.

Now buoyant upon somehow unknowable,
indiscernible seas' visions' forms I float,
and neither sleep nor awakening do I know—
my Mother's sanctuary is this sweet dream!
I feel the lateness, too, of the summer's breath,
and th' expensiveness of its fecundity.
Say among the countless feathery seeds that drift
only *one* were to land and grow...
Who would it be? —*Why, it would be you!*
—speak your handmaids in their intimacy.
Surrendering though, my soul heeds
a whispering from the Unknown: *It will be Me...*

SWEET TIME OF THE CHILDING

Now pass the loneliest days of my mute one's growth.
I, awaiting its first sounding,
appeal to you on its behalf: *Time! Time!*
Compassion is sweet time for the childing!

Spare not your hothouse heart's blessings for another,
far-off harvest, another orison;
feed all the wealth of your benevolence instead
to this one present dream, this hopeful,
shy hungering moment's hour, faithful to you in its longing,
justified in its claim to being
by your own desire's initiative: *you've* sown the seeds
that now breathe in this fecundity!

Mute one! Silent one!—say what sacred, sober
responsibility have I now but your birth?
Who, even what you are I know not!
Whence you come, whither you go—*I know nothing!*
I am the daughter of precious youth who stands here
looked upon, brimming with child!
I am a younger son and brother expectant
of that epiphanal one who shall be my friend.
And I am this child's home. I am its mother—
I, who plead for it, all pity for the morrow.
I am myself this child! I am this silent one
who its mother's pinings tastes and sufferings
swallows, appealing to you *for* her:
Time! Compassion is such sweet time for the childing!

Let your compassion spill and desire wonder!
Mother labours for you alone, my Lord.

YOUR AUTUMN HOUSE'S WINDOW

And I was ashamed,
for I saw you look upon me
there with your heart—
all a sad sweet wonder—
in the street beneath
your autumn house's window,
wherepast you sat
at home with yourself within,
and with your wife beside you,
while I, walking by,
—eh, perhaps hungry
and cold a little, and crazily
all laden with these
encumbrant over-fecundities . . .
—I turned my face away that you
might not discern
this longing and, concerned,
feel responsible for me.

INJUDICIOUS REQUEST

Shall I be hopeless with pride
that I went to one
who does not deal in shoes
for a pair of shoes,
found him to have nothing
to offer me, and, even,
to have largely been
indignant at my request—
since I spoke to him as one
unknown to himself?
Is it not I who is to blame
rather for lacking sense,
for misjudgment and disrespect
of his element—
so dissimilar to my own soul's
climate and needs?

Yet what you gave your goodness
gave freely to me.
Alas! I was still hungry and asked
again of you,
was thirsty and asked e'en
everything of you inside.
I entered your house
though was uninvited by you.
Yet I stole nothing and left
everything in good order.
Even—*once*—you smiled
at the fire I lit for warmth.

HIS VOICE WAS A CARESS

His voice was a caress
to my deep heart.
It lit, e'en unbeknownst to him,
a fire there, so subtle,
with all wholesome assumptions.

Ah! souls know the fire!
Its tendrils open walls,
long closed upon themselves,
of rooms of light;
some rooms below shimmer
where waters billow
bright, and some—
as though uplifted mightily
on massive wings—
light the roots of the eyes.

I saw all the world
illumined in that voice!
What words it spoke
mattered not, for its Word
had already delivered itself,
its heat its content—
openness
the gentle density of its belovedness.

Yet he knew nothing of all this!
I had hoped
but failed to tell.
Fires are such secret things.

ALL THESE ROOMS

Grant now this musing to unveil
the silence in which your rooms
were spoken to me.

There you called me in,
into a small space among fish
(which I have known in you before)
and all their waters, crisp and bubbling,
and special lights aglow,
and green wisps,
deep and umbrous green and radiant there.
We sat and watched there, you and I,
movement.

And I, all in wonder at this one room,
so daring among fish,
fish and lights and waters,
wisps and stone—
I asked what deeps were *not* known
by these fish
and waters' little lights and umbers.

Deeps of all these rooms, deeps
of wholesomeness,
deeps of deeping treasures not yet
given unto me.

GLEANS OFFERING

I pulled the fish up in nets from the depths
and I laid them before him—
a myriad of shivery edible jewels
glistening in the sun at his feet.

But he asked that I offer them, one by one,
from my mouth
to his panting hunger-silkèd mouth instead.

Who could have imagined
how immense a tenderness has this God
for the merest pebble-gleans of the heart's ocean?

Borrowed Wings

The hour in which the dawn broke,
in which I saw an ardent place,
I was flying—
though I knew not what
sure means I soared by.
I simply found myself aloft up high,
as though from
slumberings of years untold awaking
mid-flight on borrowed wings.

And passing low and near
to a cavern's mouth,
I looked down and in
and knew again somehow
a deep church of shimmering flames,
like heartbeats of my
many great longings,
dancing in the moving prayerful airs
of a gestation chamber
facing out to sea.
And I wanted
therein to enter and to be.

But alas! did those wings
uplift and float me
on and on without tarrying,
unheedful of the bleeding heart
I was carrying!

BEATITUDES OF THE SEA

Blessed are my ears to hear
the cry of the gulls of the sea beyond my window.
Blessed is my heart to bring forth
weeps for love of deeps that house her salt soul.
Blessed is my life to feel and breathe
the winds that carry her many whisperings.
May I never leave her side—
may she become herself my spirit's begging-bowl.

Blessed is my brokenness—
nothing have I my own in which to hold God's Love.
Helpless does it pour on me—
between my hands it runs in rivers down to the sea.
Blessed are these hands despite—
for they by waters take up anew their devotion.
They pray to never leave her side—
may she become herself these hands' purity.

And e'en the sky must testify—
and e'en the sun must witness to her clarion light.
How blessed are my eyes!—
for they shall see God's Smile glistening upon her face.
Many are the years I long to have
gifted to me, delighting in her swollen promise.
May I never leave her side—
may she become herself the womb of all my grace.

All I have ever wanted, and all I will need,
is now a treasure within her deep heavings.
Blessed is my soul's choice of her!—
in its love shall it be healed of its grievings.

SISTER SEA

O! my sister sea—beloved swollenness
and moving birth-womb of all waves, rise!
All glory of God above has touched you,
ruptured the ancient pull of your bed's ties.
You, ripped from them today, were lifted up—
and I saw you heave without sighs,
and break forth upon shores of dream that seemed
by your self-gift beyond the skies!

You spoke a longing to my heart
of the whisper of a memory's wealth long forgotten.
Lights from another place and time
you bid glint green and white upon your face.
A sea of angels' gentle fires in song
and wings' uplifting releasement by the grace
of godheads infinite you were—and a delight
in your dark deeps have they begotten.

O! my sea of greatest love, do not your insides
tremble, are you not fearful in flight?
Does not this Breath beneath your weight
so swift-impelling you to such a height,
and in your core so fixèd-willing a vast freedom's
opening and summoning might—
does it not trouble your soul, beholding none
but One dwelling in endless light?

Timid my heart is still before majesty—
timid and taut 'fore Your all-claiming call.
Yet You raised my sister to all belovedness of being—
and You did not let her fall!

THE WATERS

In this place—it is inexplicable—
is the graciousness of waters.
Someone put a breath in my heart,
and in my soul a daughter's
inborn longing. All light here
is the colour of belovedness;
and allwhere within light,
such memories swell of a tenderness
which I have yet to live.

They found me, O! God, such hopes,
when I wasn't looking for them—
fecundated futures for me,
when all my dreams lay still
hidden in the Hand which stays,
when dreams were beats
in the bosom of the Ancient of Days.

In this place—it is inexpressible—
my heart heals of its shame.
Long had it demurred before the Vast—
hung sadness its name.
But in this place the full flight of gods
is these waters' gift!
We are gods! And these waters,
e'er gracious, will give us lift!

O! my heart, take root—
take from these waters the Spirit's loam,
saying: *Count me among your lovers!*
You will find your home.

ROOT CHILD

Faded was the light on that day,
now years ago, when I planted this tree.
Longing was my heart with but one hope,
with one promise yet sorely mute.
Oft have I lamented that the sky,
the sun itself, it seemed, had heard nothing:
how I put this treasure in the earth to unfold—
and I kept watering the root.

Someone told me: *Let these young shoots
here reach forth to great heights.
See how they respond to the sweet sound
of the playing of My flute!*
Thusly did I bid them climb and bid them flower.
But He pruned them!
I choked floods into the earth of my tears—
and with them, I watered the root.

And the earth sheltered me—and I new-pledged
my treasure to Her deep grace.
I stopped hoping for a dream beyond the reach
of my heart of this tree's fruit.
I imagined worlds *beneath* the soil
in the rich black of earth's cool embrace.
But *She* whispered things unfathomable—to *Him!*
—while I watered the root.

All my love have I poured into her,
this root-child to whom my soul cleaves.
Years I noticed not how she had grown—
until you, friend, admired her leaves.

In the Garden

These are the flowers whose many fiery names
are yet hidden within God.
Strange is their fragrance at this bottom:
so dense, so complex, like food.

One who has come here long aeons
has planted them, and tends them e'en still.
His footsteps are those whose weightlessness
crushes the spirit's airy mood,
and dashes all hopes hard against themselves
which seek a blithe fulfillment,
and kills with a whisper of a compelling promise
of His advent nude.

He presses these flowers' interiors
and makes their sweet fires release,
and ravages delicate longings which any soul
aspires still softly to breathe.
He is God of all this garden.
I know not whence I came here to be kept
among its teeming shoots and seeds.
But here have I desperately wept,
and held so raw among my heart's shattered dreams
His pacings alone.

All those dreams destroyed! Pray, count them all!
And yet I cannot mourn them.
For one eve He came fragrantly so close
that He saw Himself in my mirror,
and a rife, fiery substance took shape within my soul,
and I knew who I am.

Against All Odds

What a grace does my soul e'er aspire to!—
to be bathed in the womb of the Word
where the meaning of each being is gathered in
and, as one, by the Beloved myrrhed.
My heart in steady desperation cleaves fast
to that place's threshold, dies at its door—
that something new, shy and yet self-existent,
might come to life in a fiery core.

What a wealth does my deep mind envision!—
caresses of th' essences of all things,
like fish in the sea of the infinite,
or bright birds of heaven with silvery wings,
or seedlings bursting forth from the brine.
But what is it makes all these truth-showings mine?
Is it not because the very flesh of my spirit
is given to me as their touchings' shrine?

What a hope is my heart yet aroused to!—
that a hidden Smile sunder the veil,
that all these things in which the Lord plays His game,
masks e'er insistent, yet frail,
release the tight weavings of their forms
and let His Breath be nakedly known.
Then let His Eye by penetration find only Himself
in me—yea! Himself alone!

For what a death does my soul oft imagine!—
sweet mergence in that loveliest of Gods.
All its little gifts and narrow dreams it abandons,
hungering Him alone—and against all odds!

THE BEATING OF MY HEART

To come to me
in Your nakedness—
to be throbbing raw,
to be touched—
You do not venture forth.

For shyness in
my depths You are,
and in Your steep highness
impassibly
You dwell unrevealed.

I offered to You
a whispered flower,
I begged You with
a burdened breast—
fragrant with Your absence.

But how can I woo You?
With what rustling,
irresistible gentleness
of manifold being
might You feel at home?

I have perhaps
offended Your simplicity
with the sheer
beating of my heart.

YOU HAVE THE BREATH

There is a birth my soul seeks,
a buoy, a life that I seek,
a high hope crystalized, enthroned
as my immaculate love for You.

And is that not, my Friend,
what You intend for me—
that rarest bliss-seat of homely fire,
all-warming and yet bonny-cool
and bright as stars and suns
and children who know joy?

Then why do You not believe my heart
that this is its one true longing?
Why not establish it
in its devotion-domain,
its kingdom of the peace of a life with You?

Rather, speed the hour of its gifting—*Your* hour!
And suffer the bitterness of my waiting—
and all the insults that I have
hurled upon You in my despair—
to be but little pebbles of time.

For even when I have hated You,
I never loved anything more,
and I never left You—
for You have the breath of th' immortal life.

THE CLOUDS

Has it not failed, then—this great experiment,
venture of a friendship without a mold,
hope of a true divinity shared, which was ours?

Has not that birds' flight of an afternoon's
brightest openness o'er seas and wide vistas
with sweet-scented trees with blossoms white—
has it not stuck in the mud of the earth's
cold and insatiable nighttime?

For ah! beloved, I am fallen apart in my sorrow!—
and you are, my dear, as ever,
as the sun, basking far away
and unperturbed in your own light.

Though one day in your homecoming you will
perhaps notice only thick clouds between us.
And ask yourself you will, then—and ask me,
and ask e'en the gods—why it must be so.

But who of us will have an answer?
Who of any of us will know most truly how to blow
those hope-overwhelming clouds away?

SINKHOLE

Do not fall down into
the sinkhole of consciousness.
For all the foundations now
are crumbling fast,
and though the soul knows
that it is not its own ground,
the proud mind is being humbled,
the heart,
a babe in the woods,
is so afraid of the possibilities,
and all the body knows is that
a wounding hole
has somehow become gaping
there in its deep insides.

Such myriad holes, yea,
in the earth are opening,
but the Spirit does not yet fill them
with its buttressing.
They feel like a sinkhole
in the consciousness—
into which one, even the Lord's beloved,
has fallen today.

Abyssal Prayer

No one taught me to pray like that.
I just found one day an abyssal breath
calling to me—
e'en from beyond my depths—
and I have never known my old
happiness of heart since.

Now my prayer is
a weeping and a longing unconsoled.

Though sometimes the breath leaves
crystal shards filled with a soft light
and almost whispering.
And sometimes a tender pain feeds,
though never satiates,
this heart heaving without rest.

But once, once alone, I gulped,
in deep dark,
the diamond of an other life—
vast fire within a homelessness,
smiles from beyond all reckoning,
a gift never to be held in the hand.

And always has it made my heart,
all too accustomed to the shining
idols of this world,
cleave to a namelessness shrouded
thick in the empty marrow of being.

WILDERNESS PRAYER

Give that I might always pray
in that breathless,
abyssal astoundedness of soul
'fore the God of the naked wilderness.

What tender intimacies shall be
visited to my breast,
that I might call Him familiarly,
He Himself will gift to me
in His deep silence of concern.

I shall address Him, then,
by a lenient, sweet name,
a soft balm on a child's lips,
and yet fiery
and e'er blistering to my bones.

Such is the prayer
of the child of the wilderness:
rapt in the breathing
of ten thousand seasons
having passed and still to come
and, still unknown,
harbouring the first home
of that Smile unhorizoned—
from e'er alive with a Love that,
fierce and piercing,
sobers an all too lightly laughing
human heart.

THE VOLCANO'S LISTENING

Lord, You do not shun, I think,
the deep autochthonic power.

And yet You would have it be
humble before You,
yet You would have it be
childlike and open to Your desire—
so that even a volcano's core,
rapt in its wild eruption,
were it to hear Your bidding,
should grow calm again,
and know not sorrow for missed glories,
but rest and sleep and, in sleeping,
dreaming, listening for Your summons.

For You are an enflourishing God.
Yes, You have Your hour, of course—
and all things blossom in the moment
assigned to them by You, and not before.

Ah! but that's the thing indeed so keenly
testing of the young volcano's heart!
Better not to speak of it o'ermuch!
Best to remain, without thereof thinking,
just listening.

Dark Charisma

The world is not wanting
in a wealth of new glories—
but I must treasure most
that old goodness of the ancient wind
gusting whither it wills in wide lands,
and whispering of the lungs' luxuriousness,
a sweet hallowing of the breath.

I know not whence it draws near to me,
no, nor through what infinity it roams—
but it suffers never a lack
of great radiant newnesses of its own.
For always it begins again
a golden dawn's advent in coming,
and never a dearth it knows, no,
of jewels renowned and beloved to the heart,
for it stirs and delivers my depths to love.
It draws forth children like diamonds
—whose child, too, I am.

And all the glories of this world
I must finally grasp in this blessing's light.
For whence else could they come
if not from deep rootedness of the earth
in that which is mightier still in being?
And by what means their growth
if not by wondrous ground
whose soil hosts a dark charisma,
billowing in the majesty of a Life
here tucked in the blind core
of a living seed?

EVOLUTION

Deep in my cells I remember
the emergence of green.
All the life on this earth
harbours a residual bliss
from that day of awaking,
the fresh sunrise, first solar kiss
upon lands new living,
gifted by a glorious purpose unseen.

An archetype of growth pulses,
buried in my clay base.
It feels the towering up
of all verdant things towards sky,
great trunks and tender stems
and sweet grasses spry,
reaching to that future aeon
wherewith leaps forth a face
sufficing as the image of the One
from time's dawn calling.

And yet, turned to heights,
life's response endures an old pain
of carrying a sullen support
inclining always to sleep again,
hindering the spirit's flight,
binding it to a past crawling.

An ecstasy and an agony both
is this world's path to God,
all green livings aspiring up from
and returning to sod.

REGROUNDING RAIN

These days passing
have been graced with rain.
Such is the sweet
downpour of high majesty
swiftly having set
to shivering once again
a sleeping depth's
primeval necessity

to wake up to larger Life's
own fairer fields,
and be thus filled
with love-abounding breath,
to have torn down
what stubbornly never yields
to smiles and tenderness
beyond cold death.

O! God, such paining cracks
in the foundation!
All the old plates
and stone tablets slide
and groan and shatter bitterly
from this dilation:
the pretense,
the awesome autochthonic pride

of drowsing depths
by rain so fiercely pounded—
all broken to rise up
fresh to Life, regrounded.

THE MONASTERY CHAIR

I once walked in the woods in winter
and found there a turned-over chair;
I set it aright, and bowed, and gave myself
to its provision for a thought.
And therein did I fall—as though a sudden
clearing in the woods had opened—
down into the dark abyss, the storehouse
of th' unfinished things of God.

Silt from ancient days there was, and things
that as of yet had no being,
and violence of a course which e'er drew
back to dust what it had given forth.
And yet a light expanded, too, still veiled,
and, fueled by each new articulation,
served that Master Hand whose Purpose
all this terribleness of depth keeps,
all this death, and all these heaving sleeps
and cries of a primeval need—
while every hope, be it e'er so slight,
like a jarred firefly in the night,
had its own time in that Master's Dream.

And if you asked me how in springtime
such great life comes from winter's deeps,
I'd say: "Sit upon the chair!"

I took it back to the monastery grounds;
I thanked it with a humble thanks,
and placed it next to another, like to itself,
overlooking the stream.

In My Grandfather's House

There came of late an autumn eve
when longing filled my heart to go
to live in light, away for a while
in the House of my Grandfather.

His harvests were rich ones always
—this was my faithful trust—
and earth-sweet and pungent
with the deep movements of mind.
His gathering delved to roots,
uncovered growth's secret origins
in dark places, so that hungerings
to be soil myself for living thought
therewith found their best food.

To be apprenticed in nurturing
in the wide fields of understanding
and copious dream I purposed,
watered by His long concern.
For I remember years ago how
His strength, His power gently
cradled the fragility of my soul—
a babe to be a god one day,
a seed to be a tree fruit-laden,
a flowering meadow to be free.

And I find a fragrance of my own
there in my Grandfather's House,
there under His husbandry
—yea! this is my faithful trust—
when He brings His harvest home.

THE HUSBANDMEN

We Adams of this hour—
lustering, visionful hour—
we are the husbandmen of the Supreme.
We plough a malleable soil
in the wide, skyey bright
fire-fields of His infinite Dream.

Once borne upwards by
earth's own natural thrust,
borne now higher by an ethery delight,
we bear the earth ourselves
within us as our abyss
ingathering towards our height.

And with esteem for all this world—
land but newly seeded,
though harbouring harvests of the Beyond—
we cultivate the Real
that is His Breath in all space,
His timelessness in each day dawned,

yea! Love that holds
all these veritables in being,
and we upraise them Him to please.
And ever is the grace of our work
to us a heart's holy joy,
for it has gifted us the Kingdom's keys.

OF DANCING AIR

There is a true and verdant wind which blows
robust, a fissure forcing within my mind;
it reaches down to depths and there shows,
in pulsing glimpses, a bright Kingdom's repose,
and opens onto pastures whose threshold
is scarcely yet crossed by humankind,
whose fragrance, rife and deep and bold
and sweetening all dreams with living gold,
sets the air dancing 'neath a measureless sky,
and thusly calls its inhabitants to live.

These dwellers there, they move so nigh,
and yet so far in pastures beyond our sigh.
But I can hear their voices on the wind,
and guess their thrill at the dawn; and high,
and ever higher in their noontide's great sea,
I reach for some smallness of their intimacy,
ungraspable to us in whole, chagrined
as we are this side of daybreak's panoply
which sets the air dancing 'neath a bountiful sky,
and thusly calls its inhabitants to give.

Who are they, these firstborn of the Kingdom?
And do they even know it yet in full sun?
For though already born into their wingdom,
from high springs drinking, in deeps well-swum,
their eyes freely beholding glories bright,
their feet apace beyond all joyless night,
yea! though breathing a single Breath as one,
their hearts are still so tender and slight
compared to air dancing 'neath that everlasting sky
under which the Son of Man will forgive.

THE KING'S BOWER

A one who's King in ruby robes,
whose garden is a fecund bower
in which I won that love which probes
the hidden depths of His high tower—

I know I'll meet Him there once more,
our spirits' loam as though infused
in one another's tender core.
My heart, once doleful, now's enthused

with breathing widened far beyond
my former penury's of wood.
Such wings upon a vagabond!—
I once, by grace unhoped-for, stood,

with flowers stolen, 'fore that King!
He wooed my trembling breast to sing!

THE TASK

E'er sweet was the dream that I had,
like a seed having burst from its pod,
that the righteous delight of my soul
was the leg of the throne of God.

Not a foot nor the seat nor an arm
nor a part but the leg front and left.
And it bore such a weight as the Infinite,
though its core was a gap and bereft,

and as though to be splintered each instant,
yet sustained by an all-knowing Eye
and a Voice that caressed deep the hollow
of my soul's sun, all to glorify.

It said: *This one, whose devotion is writ,*
is cut stone for the task of completing it.

STANDING STONE

Your Love is a regnant standing stone.
From deeps within a quickening core
has it arisen, roots unknown—
an adamant ambassador

of timeless promises of dream
more waking still than open eyes,
of deeds of will of the Supreme
to blossom forth a paradise!

O! fecund vigor of inner suns—
you wound delectably this earth!
O! children, lovely blessed ones
whose mother, by this stone, gave birth,

do not you see?—this stone is living!
Become, then, hearts of sweet thanksgiving!

To the Past Ones

So many centuries have passed between us!
Yet have all been graced this bliss—
that secret whispers dewed and glorious
rapt-compose all souls, and kiss

and render poised these very same in joy.
For counting centuries' years as naught,
as if all aeons' breadth were His darling toy
and tender playthings those He caught,

like stars of a sumptuous dream-rich world,
or sun-drunk flowers of endless morn,
little precious boats with their sails unfurled,
God calls each one His own firstborn,

and gifts to each its life from before all ages,
deeming worldly whiles but scribbling.
And thus to you from teeming history's pages
cries my soul: Yea! you are my sibling!

Two Trees

I stand between
two trees of the living breath—
shining persons veiled
in an old foresty magnificence.

One is before me;
the other is behind, cradling
my aspirations in its sweet wood,
my flesh in its shade,
a lover and the guardian
of my roots' density—

while I face up
to the blossoming one I must climb.

LOST CHILDHOOD

We have given birth to one another,
once more, you and I,
my good blossom of my heart,
my vibrant love and garden.

Deep your sweet delight is in me,
whom I call my faithful husband,
bright of eye in my life's bud
which you now gently unharden,

and smiling in my vision of our dawn's
own tenderest first light,
and healing and forgiving
of that naught-wound that was my pain,

willing into being the happy wealth
of a lost ancient childhood
wherein we, clothed in a flowering nakedness,
drank the rain.

The Husband

Let my husband come to me now—
we have for so long a time been far apart.
I'd forgotten how I knew him once so well
just by the scent of his breath within my heart,
and by those full, deepening moves in me
which e'er spoke in silence a great intimacy,
his eyes for me so wholly smiling always
with the promise of a future's fecundity.

I don't remember now how we first met—
nor for what purpose I left him, nor when I did.
Yet e'er have I been looking for him since
in all places wherein his love's traces hid.

And I've found that he's been true to me—
he's been patient with my many restless scenes.
And long has he desired another rendezvous
with me in those deep ravines
where e'er we used to walk and sit and laugh
and speak of all manner of things,
and heave up stones and drink therefrom
the cool sweets of our ownmost natures' springs.

And once into the stream we stepped.
Ah! beloved!—'twas e'er the same stream,
though flashings from the form-play of the infinite
poured o'er our heads, tumbling as in a dream.
For you and I were naked and in love so deep
we touched the bottom and it became the sky,
and all else did we find there as each other,
and we were married as are gods—*without a why!*

SUSPENSION

He caught me up full in His Hand this day,
sustained all my being without feet on the ground.
Not weightless was I; my weight was a substance
not mine, but continuous with creatures all round:

a liquid-light consciousness shaped by the Will
of a Person unseen yet whose nature is Love,
a gossamer holding that weaves all in dream,
deep delight which has neither a ceiling above

nor a floor at the bottom nor walls to enclose
static places constructed by mind's busy toil.
A fluid spontaneous Life was that swimming
suspendedness cradled in ethery soil.

And all ways I turned I could see only Him;
in the faces of creatures His own eyes abide.
'Twas a taste of sweet timelessness destined to dim—
for so will He show Himself naked, then hide,

yea! flaunt His own Beauty in spiritual flesh,
then cover Himself in the rags of the world.
He does this to fire up the heart in my breast
in a longing dilated, like a sail unfurled

in the wind. For alas! is my heart still so small;
and thus does He raise me, then drop me, then call
yet again. But I know not what day we'll next meet,
nor the hour in which I'll need no longer my feet.

OF STARS AND ETHER

A star from heaven falling
I beheld when skyward gazing;
it stirred in me the calling
of my life, to sing in praising
the Beloved's Name. O! clinging
is my heart in endless longing
for glorious and sweet ringing
of that Name in wondrous songing.

A star in heaven burning
gifts my heart its wings for flying;
I soon shall see returning
to me tears that I've been crying
as showers of grace downpouring.
O! to stars shall I be soaring
through ether, echoing His Name!

NIGHT SKY

Once when I felt loved by You
I saw the night sky open its abyss
and reach down to my depths
to know me,
face to face to be mine only
to beckon me beyond my sorrow.

Yet not beyond the world to beckon—
rather vigorously more into it.
For so my depths were its depths too,
and it was beckoned in me by You,
ordained to the same delight-stuff
as Your smile.

No, not beyond the world to beckon—
but more to the perfection of its hope,
to the intimacy prepared for long
by the very darkness of its seed:
forgotten always in mute winter,
rumouring awakening in the spring's dawn,
and there, gaping as a summer's night sky,
breathing Your love.

THE SEAGULLS

This morning are the seagulls' soarings
gloriously songful!
So let them sign a day of breathful,
uplifting delight!

Yet e'er is there a sadness-tinge within
their throatiness of cry
which whispers of this world's abyssal
cleaving to that height,

and yearns a deep acknowledgment
from shining worlds above
which even seagulls' soarings fail
to fathom but in dream.

O! let their songs inspire me! Let my mind
take up their wings!
For I know well their sadness. I know not
their flight's regime.

NOTHING HAS BEEN LOST

Once when you were very young in this life,
I came again to see you.
Many years I've led you since,
secretly winding your path to bring you home.
And all along the way you've gathered
noiseful bits of the world's tome,
and found yourself at last in a forest
tangled with much for you to do,
a clutter of structures of thought and voices
annexing your mind—and yet, too,
longing to renew our love in open spaces,
removed from the gloam.

Now sit very near to Me
and wait upon the gift of My choice deed.
I will be the calm for you for a little while,
for your soul is restless.
Till silence you welcome into your heart deeply,
it will feel guestless.
But when there flourishes a space for Me inside,
like the empty reed,
My sun will blaze within you
and prosper there gloriously every seed,
and no golden bird of joy will find itself
lost in your life, nestless.

Beloved, it is true that you and I together
have still so very far to climb.
Yet lament not—in all your wanderings without Me,
nothing has been lost but time.

PILLOWS FOR KUSUMITA

A late afternoon
in a half waking dream
some years ago
while visiting you in your house,
a sweet moment hovering
on the cusp of worlds
revealed to me
a delicate citizen of the inner ether.

She was floating without wings,
poised upright
a foot off the floor,
robed in wisps of white,
and she had humble little fingers,
busy gathering,
or so it seemed to me,
pillows' essences
from the furniture
near which I drowsed.
She was bringing them
down the hall to you,
back and forth to your room,
the while she smiled.

I said, intrigued, to her:
"What are you doing?"
And she: "I am bringing
pillows for Kusumita."
"Who are you?" I inquired then,
her eyes meeting with mine.
"I am here to serve Kusumita."

And that was it—
her whole identity defined
by service that was gifted to her
in a dimension unseen
by the full waking eyes and mind.

And this, more than floating,
soft essences in hand,
more than seeing her at all there,
was the marvel—
so that my wondering being
sought to rouse itself
to think upon
this perfection of self-offering
that was hers.
But when it did so, she was gone.

The grasping mind
knows not the delicacies
of the subtle inner worlds.
Yet you, my friend,
I believe, are well tended to
by one of its citizens.

Like a Heartbeat

I sat today
on the branch of the tree
where you rested in June
when we walked together.

I can still see the picture in my heart,
though I hold it,
my friend, not too tightly.

Like a heartbeat,
I let it go and come again
to throb inside in bright glory—
for so might I grasp
just a little more of your love—
and let it fade once more
like these September leaves.

And then it throbs again,
my good memory gracing—
for unlike these leaves evanescing,
my heart keeps beating.

REBECCA'S LITTLE LOVE

I see my little Jacob child
running there in the tender breezes;
the sun shines golden upon his hair
with utter privilege so openly to touch him.
The light within his eyes and smile
a singularity gifts to my vision.
O! my little love, I loose these fetters gently
and stand to watch you.

Would that I was your sister young;
you would comfort me from my dark fears.
Would that I was your sister elder;
you would run to me from your own.
A mother, though, to be of such abyssal sweetness
is high for my small heart.
If you do not belong to our God,
surely all your bright limbs must be orphaned.

When you are old in my morrow's night,
I will not see your dear face.
And when comes your hour of choice,
I know not to whom you will offer your dreams.
Yet this gem here carved in me by your present
will endure beyond our last parting.
Perhaps your hands do not yet hold it,
but I know you fathom its secret.

O! my little Jacob pilgrim,
do not misplace my gem with its many a facet;
perhaps one glint from it one rare day
will bless your life with power to surpass it.

Two Kings

Quickened is my songful heart to the new day,
this waxing before dawn, by two kings.

One is a king of all blossoming sweet flowers;
he has for myriad ages spawned to its teeming
from a dark charisma here within my mind
the garden of my most intimate play and feelings;
he hides from me oft and teases, and I adore him.

The other is the dweller of the heights as yet
unreachable as a sun beyond all ages of the world;
he, the worshipped and the feared one, pours down
an unquenchable light upon my soul—
wherefore oft do I see my flowers die.

And yet I need them both, these two kings.
For life without my high king is incomplete
and vain in the recklessness of its fecundity;
yet lo! without my sweet king and his smile
I live intolerably as in naked flame.

But so sounds nevertheless the high king's claim:
that destiny of my dark ground, soon to be
illumined and splayed by his own fiery name.

O! how, then, shall my flowers grow—
in what loam of the king who loves me sweetly,
yea! and also smiles perhaps only because
there are seeds' secrets hidden in me still in deep soil?

MIND'S PYRE

In my youth my mind flew high,
and it extended out
searching fingers of desire
hungering, O! for knowledge—

at which, my Lord, You smiled,
and You blew my heart
a wounding kiss of love
unlooked-for, and devastating.

Like a bird shot
suddenly in the breast
by a well-aimed arrow
at a distance beyond reckoning,
and all that winged one's life
fell in ruins—

so, too, all that I had hungered for
turned to a monument of vanity,
and I felt Your smile thereafter
as a burning fire in the wound.

And yet it was
unearthly fire, unconsuming,
a beauty afore unshown,
the one thing now to be known.

Your deep delight is in me, Beloved,
undoing all I am, and yet I live.
Your smile chars my house to cinders,
and yet my house stands.

What is it that I hunger for now
if not for Your hands full of fire?
To what does my mind send out its fingers
if not to its pyre?

FLOWERS OF FIRE

Why do You ask me, Love,
for my heart-flowers
when You know—
all too well You know!—
that I have none now?

You said Yourself to me once—
oh, You did!—
not unsolemnly:
"I put you, O! My dear one, My pup,
too soon into the fire."

And do You wonder that
in fire alone it is now
that I most hunger for You?

I offered You once
my fragrant vineyards.
Ah! I was so young then.
Do not ask me now to replant
a scorched garden.

All things I burn down, my Love—
unless, too, by Your good will,
I learn to cultivate for You
a heart hot and full
with flowers of fire.

CHINMOY THE BLUE BIRD

Chinmoy the blue bird flew here once
in my mind and made my vision smile.
Sweet was the scent my eyes knew,
and blue their bliss-covenant with sky.

Space, billowing, embraced him—
reality's intensive infinities bloomed.
And therein his fleet wings traced shapes—
scripts, dreams of a desire born, dreams
dream-born blue in a lover's heart's womb.
From the Unknown, called forth, worlds came,
begot, as though from naught to full plume,
lovely blue—and in his billowing name
I might have asked anything and received.

Chinmoy the blue bird, white-breasted.
That my heart's breath knew such joy!
O! that my heart, too, were Chinmoy!
This I asked, this above all, this at once!
That, and this, too—that here, someday,
the billowing blue-deep sea might fly, too!

SMALL HOUSE

When in dark night You
visited my house and entered inside,
and I didn't ask You, nor cared,
whence You had come to me,
but rather, like a child, I took at once
You to be mine alone,
then were You truly well-pleased,
forgetting Your own Name.

Lord, we were two bosom friends
free in our blooming youth.
Lord, we ate sweets and honeycomb,
and You kissed my eyes.
You planted word-treasures
like little songs in the garden.
But still a wound persisted in me
which cried for deepening.

I wanted not this carefree friendship
always inside my house.
I wanted fire to burst forth blazing,
even from our laughter.
I wanted no more house,
but vastness of a white-fire infinite,
and therein an angel's blow
to shatter my deeps' long longing.

And I wanted silence to betray to me
Your most naked Name,
and, clothed in its nakedness,
to be welcomed as Your Beyond!

Should all the heavens stand amazed
at a small heart's boldness?
O! nay, Lord! For You Yourself
elected it in my tiniest room!

GOLDEN BELL

O! harken, my heart,
to that great golden bell
which once reposed
silently cold in the deeps:

how all my undying desire
had hunted it,
all the voluptuous grasping
of my hungry mind

had striven to heave up
and then to enshrine it
in temples on high
by its knell first unfolding—

but was, by its weight like a planet,
prevented,
so never its ringing, my heart,
had you heard,

till one eve our Lord in His love-play
crept by us
adorned in its tinkling,
the bell ornamenting His ear.

TREE OF MY YOUTH

A towering tree
with sweet pine branches
conducted me to Your sky
in my nimble youth.
The clouds that day
in whirling dances
let blaze in halting displays
Your sun of truth.

Yet billowing was
my heart in hope
that on the breeze my longing
might unhindered rise,
and to Your hearing
make deep appeal
in wordless prayers
and with hunger in my eyes.

I was above
all other trees there;
no higher could I go
by bright green earthly means.
My soul in strainèd striving
sought to fly
and enter the delight
of Your high heavenly scenes.

And in my will's extension
You saw me,
and made me to be a one
who would search long years
to discover inside of myself

Your hiding place
that we might be for one another
living mirrors.

DOOMSDAY TREE

This day in my garden, in a golden evening, I planted a tree.
Now let it be a symbol to my heart
of a deep trust in Your loving investment of this world.

For too few have the vision in this late hour
to commence a firm commitment to so lengthy a growth.
Yea! too few have that wide strength of soul
to will a future better than ours for those not yet living.
And too few hope truly and so truly believe that,
by Your grace, this world will continue in its being.

But the Prophet said: "If Doomsday comes and finds you
with a sapling in your hand, it should be planted."

Yea! plant the tree, because You, O! Merciful One,
can fill up the last hour's emptiness with infinity,
can make to flourish and bloom and give fruit
a tree—my tree that I planted—though it be engulfed in flames.

ANGEL IN THE STORM

The storm has begun.
Thus says the angel of the Lord,
that now the fire of your rising life
struggles in the smoke,
and the fuel all through is water-soaked
and sputtering and grave,
and there is dankness
in your mind's becoming,
your eye is dull as folk
long worked to the bone
without a hope of joy.

Yet child, says he, you are the Lord's toy!
Come in now
out of this great tumult of the wind!
For the Lord hears your heart's prayer,
He knows your longing,
and Heaven does not say
that you have sinned.

Rather are some things kept always
under the deep concealing cloak
of Love's gentleness.

Lo! your bright life still does thrive.
For He is Lord over storms,
and you are thoroughly blessed,
sheltered and alive, and are His daughter,
close to His Bosom pressed.
Come in now, O! beloved of His Heart,
out of this inclement, wild water!

UNDER THE BRIDGE

I've heard Your footsteps coming to me
under the soaring bridge of my life.
Up on its high top is the pathway to glory
brightly illumined by your sun.

Yet beneath it You now walk in shadow,
for there I have taken up my abode
in a cold, lightless squalor of low dreams
born in the mud of an ancient ignorance.

Ah! they come close to me, those footsteps,
without a judgment upon my heart.
Having fallen with a misstep from the edge,
I tumbled down under the bridge.

And down they came, too, to uphold me,
we two in the mire and the gloom together.
I heard them laughing there just this eve,
wonderfully delight-filled even in the nether.

STANDING STEW

Here at the ongoing
banquet that is my life
is an ever sumptuous
standing stew served.

The Lord cooks with
what ingredients He has,
and as I eat in my hunger,
He adds more to it;
and I add, too, my own
at times, and He seasons
to off-set them, if they are
ill-chosen flavours.

And thus am I fed
each day by His compassion,
and by His dream
that I be His eagle-child.
And though we've yet
to realize the golden recipe
for full flight—rejoice!
My soul does not despair!

For I hear Him singing
in the kitchen there,
bright with His apron on,
trying out new herbs,
and with the stew still
bubbling on the stove.

THE WAGON RIDE

Of late I have been riding
in the wagon of the Lord.

He found me like a child
having run away from home,
having fallen in the mud,
having sullied all my diamonds.

O! yes, I still had diamonds in my pocket,
and now with them
I'm paying for the wagon ride
to the great sea of my dreams.

And yet with every mile of road,
the Lord's wagon, it seems,
itself is as the great sea to my heart,
glistening with suns.

For lo! for every diamond that I give,
to Him as mere crumbs,
He gives to me so many more,
and far more beautiful ones.

FORGIVEN BY DIAMONDS

Who was he to show me that I had hidden
rich treasuries just bristling with folds of diamonds?
Someone that Your Hand had claimed in secret
to break open and flourish my innermost heart!

For though he knew it not, his gentle voice
a salty resonance commenced within me,
and chambers soft as sea-foamed fissures
swiftly were dilated onto wide sky above,
and veils upon my brow were thinned,
and stars mirrored as gifts in the unfathomable deep,
their light a piercing, as though a patience
of long incalculable years steadily called.

And whole harvests of glistenings, high ancient breaths,
bejeweled fish, an astonishing eye,
and emptiness receiving my full-winged joy
ravished my world, birthed a habit of song in me.

And smiles pursued my lips by day,
and tears my tender heart-thrills in nighttime.
And futures You bestowed through him!
O! heartily You used him, until I mistook him for You!

Still, Lord, no harm in this—for You triumphed!
My innermost heart now flourishes in Your Name!
And as for his offense at my exorbitant gratitude,
his own diamonds will have forgiven me.

HIDE AND SEEK

Then came a night
on which You suddenly became—
O! whole inner worlds
setting spinning in Your zeal—
host of a happy game
of hide and seek in my house,
and I found You there
already about inside, tiptoeing.

And I soon forgot
all the old empty, small hours,
for now my rooms were
living as a flowering palace's,
with graced gold and
sweet fullnesses to befriend me.

And space's deep dilation You gave,
opening air's flesh
to fresh and endless moments of time,
that You might
playfully discreet yourself,
like sweet whisperings of angels,
in the billowing folds of ether.

High Winds

I climbed up but a single step—
a lone step up
to a sweet, long hungered-for vista—
and I found there,
O! that, Love, without Your buoyancy
every moment
billowing up my diminutive life,
I fall down,
down many steps of ease long surpassed,
tumbling.

The elements no longer support me,
as they used.
Long floated I in the Mother's womb,
ages uncounted.
But this day I am born and naked
in high winds.

O! let that great Love protect me, then,
in this new clime.
For vigorous tempests rage round me—
and though my head be
in the sunlight, yet my lungs, opening
to boundless breath,
inhale the world as a tiny babe does,
vulnerable in dream.

LITTLE COTTAGE

I live a life that is but
a fragile little cottage in the wind,
with storms aswirl about it,
and a gaping earth beneath it,
and fires' great tapestries of undoing
ornamenting the sky above.

And yet my cottage stands still,
for it is built upon sure stone—
adamant to which the angels sing in choir,
deep heart breathing in ethers higher
than the atmosphere of this world,
and by whose graces all my rooms
are spaces golden with peace.

For no cottage founded on that stone
will ever see its life in light cease,
though outside destruction looms.

MEDITATION ROOM

A black storm, a whirlwind,
outside these walls wails.
But in Your hand this room
is a city on a hilltop shining.

Voices with teeth and venom
madly drive the spinning gales.
But by Your strength this room
lifts to heaven earth's pining.

Though all the noxious hate
of demons worlds assails,
yet inside this room our hearts,
to downpouring grace inclining,
sing above the tempest's trails,
dream-dawns of peace designing.

He Will Ask Me

A world is coming towards me
in which I will have no longer
any of my friends.

A day will see its dawn
on which I will wake to find
all the former ties removed.

Yet He to whom I owe my life
will ask me to remain
a while more for His pleasure—

for something in my body's form
is birthing a personal immortality
in love with Him,
and the work is slow and difficult.

O! Love, let not this mother die
before the child is born.

My Heart in Which to Live

The word
which I have waited for
these long many years
has been spoken.

The balm
has been poured out
and worked into my hopes
that were broken.

The door
that once was closed,
and I before it in bitterness,
is wide open.

I have only
to walk through,
to give to this light-filled dream
that has woken

my heart,
whose intimacy is a gift and breath
to that Lover supreme,
in which to live.

OF HOLES AND BREATH

The hole in my back
where my wings must take root
and the foundation poured be
for life everlasting,

agape in the hunger
of earth's rolling aeons
evolving the high life
of Spirit's surpassing—

Love, plant Your seed therein
and stir up the hollow's air.
For nothing sure can grow there
without Your breathing.

MY PORTION

Come, come and stand,
O! high angel of the Lord,
stand upon these idle shoulders
bowed in sorrow.

Let me be aware
of your bright wings moving
in the marrow of my being
as a new tomorrow

bustling and sweet
with the Lord's promises fulfilled,
as the hour in which He
speaks aloud to my heart

that one deep Word that,
like a deed of soaring power,
calls forth creation in magnificence,
whole and part,

and gives to me a portion,
saying, "My love, make art!"

Night Angels

The sweet hands
of beckoning angels,
one night,
so as to take me up to see You,
tried to pull me
from my body in my bed,
but I would not go!—
for, being lifted up,
I felt my root-bulb
being left behind,
and that treasure in its garden,
as which my immortality is growing,
I will not lose!

They have to know, these angels,
that I hope for no heaven
without my godhead.
O! they have to,
for Your sake, Love,
realize
that with my godhead,
heaven is wherever I am.

So let me lie in my bed, I said,
at night in peace,
you bright servants of the Lord!
For He Himself often
comes down to me in dreams
to water my loam.

ICONS IN FLIGHT

You sent me blessings
in the wings and the flight
of a flock of birds emerging
from a tree's picture
in the close intimacy of my room.

Lo! that a round thing might
take birth by Your will
from an image lacking depth!
Yet many did so,
and the tree burst into bloom.

How much more might I
expect, then, to see Your glory
in this world issuing forth
from full-bodied icons—
infinity from a sparrow's womb!

And there within that
greatest depth might I not
find the One I long for,
Your Eye smiling with the
birds, shining inside each plume?

Then shall I fall upon my
knees in gratitude for
tenderness and Your mighty grace
to have gifted me
Your secret Life to consume.

MASQUERADE

Sometimes impish Life in this world
masquerades itself
as a temporary staving off
of death's leaden regime.

This it does with honed persuasion
by sundry means:
by great strength
(one's deep own or of that another),
by good chance, by
high blessing (or appearance thereof).

But there is also dogged will
that comes to disbelieve
Life's skillful dissemblances,
as mere guiles up the sleeve,

and thus rejects its mask,
refuses the authority of death,
takes as its task
to hunt out and win that wide breath
billowing out all space
to make room for infinity.

And then Life laughs, having been
caught naked in its divinity.

TASTE OF ETHER

She had not always been,
by birth or by breeding,
destined for friendship
with the singing ether.

But You have made her so—
gave to her tender
moving airs on the inside,
though nothing had she known
of breathing without lungs,
of hearing, seeing with organs
unfleshed, yet shapely,
weighted and discrete
as new seats come into being.

Mightn't it be said of her, then,
one day, "We knew not
that she was so sweet-tongued,
that air itself had wings!"

For when they behold her there
singing of You in her heart,
they, too, will taste ether
with tongues fashioned by angels.

SUBTLE PURSUIT

Her body lies there sleeping now,
and yet her heart bright walks awake
all throughout the quieted house.

Her eyes unfluttering are and closed,
and yet she searches for You, Beloved,
inside every one of her rooms.

The playful twittering of beings
that live and have their duties near You,
she hears with ears other than those
that rest on the pillows of her bed.

A new seat has she assumed of late,
and by her will unwavering is it moved.
But still she does not find You,
even herein that subtler ether of her house.

For You, O! Beloved, hide Your face
in every world in which life breathes
from the pursuit of Your lovers!

Perhaps even now You are,
as she passes into the garden through
a window on a night without a moon,
upstairs hiding beside her sleeping body.

ALL THE BEINGS

May all the beings live in peace.
May stars delight their eyes upturned,
and twilight, with the calm's increase,
deliver them from all they've learned

that aids them not in loving You,
that, like a storehouse filled with noise
of images and tasks to do,
diminishes the spirit's poise.

Yea! creatures all may silence bless
and, deep as black behind stars' light,
may such a blessing yield no less
than peace descending from Your height

to dwell in every heart of earth,
to slow the pace and fill each hour
with potencies of priceless worth
and fragrances from every flower,

and finally the dream made real
of this world its truth bestowed.
May all the beings, then, wonder feel
and gifts receive of own abode.

O! Master, may death's cold sway cease.
May icy hardnesses be thawed,
that all the beings might live in peace,
and in that peace realize God.

A DAY AS LONG

That day was as long
as the sea, my Love.

I remember how You
well loved lingering, how all
our souls were up high flying
in Your light's laughter,
how the sky became wide
in marking the hours.

It was as long as the rain,
and the stones beneath it,
and the sun and moon above it,
and still You
poured into vessels,
all too hopeless at holding much,
all that You had to give—

until I said to You:
"O! God, this day is long as ages!"
And You smiled.

CURVATURE

I woke from a dream
and I thereupon felt,
without recalling it,
that for a long time
I had been away somewhere.

I had been secret at a distance
above, not subject
to the gravity of the earth;
perhaps an other life I had lived
in a few unknowing hours.

The dream left my sanctuary
full of the fiery atoms
of someone else's world.

And each hour afterwards,
until I slept again
in earth's bosom,
my legs wanted to walk
a straight road back there—
but I kept falling down
into the curvature of the earth.

And all the while
the custodians of my sanctuary
kept the door open—
busy at the task
of assimilating the atoms.

THE LAST THING

The last thing
at the end of the path
that you will be called upon
to let go of
is your longing.

You will be invited
to open to a life of joy—
and that is a hard thing,
the most bewildering and
precocious of invitations
to arrive: a one that
gifts to one what it invites to,

but only when the hands
have stopped clinging,
the heart cleaving,
and when the mind forgets
what all these years
it has faithfully constructed
for the heart to long for,
like an idol of stone.